# MADE
## BY
# GOD

## TONY EVANS

### Artwork by CHRISTAN STEWART

HARVEST KIDS

**HARVEST HOUSE PUBLISHERS**
EUGENE, OREGON

The quote of Acts 17:26-28 is from the Holy Bible, New International Version®, NIV®. Copyright © 1973, 1978, 1984, 2011 by Biblica, Inc.® Used by permission. All rights reserved worldwide.

Cover design and hand-lettering by Kristi Smith—Juicebox Designs
Interior design by Left Coast Design

**Made by God**
Text copyright © 2021 by Tony Evans
Illustrations copyright © 2021 by Christan Stewart
Published by Harvest House Publishers
Eugene, Oregon 97408
www.harvesthousepublishers.com

ISBN 978-0-7369-8444-7 (hardcover)
ISBN 978-07-369-8445-4 (eBook)

Library of Congress Control Number: 2021934118

**Printed in China**
21 22 23 24 25 26 27 28 29 / LP / 10 9 8 7 6 5 4 3 2 1

Do you know what you and every
other kid in the whole world shares?

All of you are made in the image of God.
God's special stamp is on *all* of you
—the stamp that says,

"Made by God—with love."

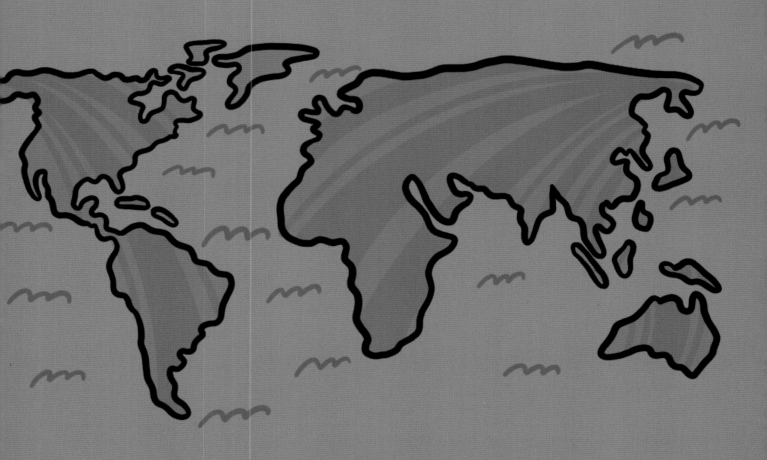

Even though everyone in the world
looks different from each other,
we are all equally made by God.

Some kids have dark skin.
Some kids have brown skin.
Some kids have light skin.

Some kids have green eyes.
Some kids have brown eyes.
Some kids have curly hair.
Some kids have straight hair.

God made us all different—we have *diversity.*

But He also made us part of the same family—
we have *unity.*

God loves and values *all* of us.

And He expects all of us to love
and value each other!

God doesn't want His children
to be mean to each other.

He wants us to be kind to everyone, no matter
what color their skin is or where they live
or what they have or don't have.

Because God loves us so much, He sent
His Son, Jesus, to show us who God is.

Jesus loved everyone the same, even if they
were poor, sick, or from a different country.

Then, because Jesus loves everyone in the world so much, He died on a cross for all the bad things, all the mean things, we have done to each other.

And three days later, Jesus rose again to defeat sin and defeat death!

Sadly, some people think they are better than others because of the color of their skin or how they look or where they're from.
This sin is called *racism.*

And racism is always, always wrong.
It hurts God's heart.
And it should also hurt our hearts.

God loves all of us *the same.*
And we should all love each other *the same.*

It all starts with *you.*
You can reach out to someone new and say,

That's what God
wants all of us to do.
*To love one another.*

God wants us to get to know many people—
not just people who look like us or dress
like us or talk like us or live in the
same kind of houses we live in.

You can find another kid who is different from you—a kid with a different color of skin, a kid from a different neighborhood, or a kid who is from another country.

Invite that kid to sit with you
during lunch at school.

Go to the park and play Frisbee.

Celebrate a birthday or holiday together.

God wants His people—the church—
to do the hard work of changing our world.
That means standing up for what is
right and true and good.

When we see racism happening,
we need to say, "This is not right.
We need to treat everyone the same.
We need to love each other.
*All* of us are precious to God!"

We need to speak words of love and kindness, not words that are mean or hateful.

If everyone did this, our world would be a safer place for everyone. All people—of all races—would feel like they matter.

Because they *do* matter.

God says so—and what God says is always true.

We can start changing our world by praying...

*God, I'm sorry.
I haven't always been
kind to others. When someone
looks different from me, I haven't
seen them as You see them—as
one of Your children, just like me.
Thank You for helping me to
love and respect everyone.
Amen.*

Next, you can stand up for what is right.

When you see something that is wrong—
like someone being treated differently because
of how they look or where they're from—
say something.

You can make a sign and put it in your window.

You can go to a peaceful protest with your family.

You can write letters to the leaders of your church, your community, and your country.

Let people know you care about the things God cares about.

When we follow God and treat others
the way He treats us—with love and kindness—
we will see God do incredible things.

The world will start to look the way He created it to look—a world of people with different colored skin and hair and eyes. A world that reflects what heaven will look like in the end.

One day, Jesus will return and make a new earth with no sin, no meanness, no racism.

Every type of person—from every country, speaking every language—will live in peace, praising God together as one united, gloriously diverse world.

"From one man he made all the nations, that they should inhabit the whole earth; and he marked out their appointed times in history and the boundaries of their lands. God did this so that they would seek him and perhaps reach out for him and find him, though he is not far from any one of us. 'For in him we live and move and have our being.' As some of your own poets have said, 'We are his offspring.'"

**Acts 17:26-28**